KHUSHI SHAH

WAR ZONE

AF529441

BlueRose Publishers

First Published in February 2021

ISBN: 978-93-5427-432-9

BLUEROSE PUBLISHERS

www.bluerosepublishers.com

info@bluerosepublishers.com

+91 8882 898 898

Cover Design:

Joshua Freitas

Typographic Design:

Namrata Saini

Distributed by: BlueRose, Amazon, Flipkart, Shopclues

Preface

I believe that one of the most crucial factors that drove me to write about my experiences in the form of this book is a realisation that dawned upon me while I was casually writing a poem on a Tuesday afternoon three months ago. It was the fact that we are all bound together by the tragedy of the occurrence of the same events and the only distinction is the execution of those events; we are all consumed by the same imbalance of pep and pain and are dubiously trying to figure out how to not let one sentiment overthrow the other. I feel that regardless of how different our stories might be, we tend to relate to each other at some point or the other and I think that's quite beautiful. But mainly, this book is a tribute to all those that contributed to the breaking as well as the making of the person that I am today, and that is what has been my greatest motivation to write about both my experiences and figments of my imagination altogether. It has undoubtedly been a difficult journey; there were times when I ran out of inspiration as well as determination, times when I couldn't muster up the courage to talk about certain experiences even when I wanted to, times when I had various conflicts with myself regarding this entire book itself, but above everything, it has been one of the most exquisite and greatest moments of my life, which I am forever going to be grateful for.

I hope that as you read the narration of my mind from here onwards, you feel at ease knowing that you are not alone, and that no matter how bad times get, the good days will indisputably arrive to compensate for the former.

Acknowledgements

I would like to express gratitude, deep from my heart towards BlueRose, my publishing house for providing me with this incredible platform and opportunity and my parents for being a constant support in every path and direction that I have chosen. I would also like to distinctly appreciate Isha and Jay for helping me conquer hindrances, for being there for me throughout this journey, and for being a rock-solid pillar all along.

Lastly, I would sincerely like to thank every person, because of whom I fell down and learned the necessary lessons for me to be able to write about it, and every person, who has been a happy memory in my life, for me to able to look at the brighter side of things too.

Contents

Introduction

A warzone, also known as a battlefield, is an area where a battle tends to take place.

And my mind and my body are a warzone, where I fight battles with, and for myself.

Here upon, it is strictly a journey of chaotic peace and brutal love.

The way I drown myself into this ocean of words and seek haven there, I hope you do too.

HURT

A Symbol of Our Love

Our love was just like a dandelion; a small, white dandelion

So beautiful and so pleasing, yet so delicate and flimsy

That even a small stroke of wind could make its blossoms fly away

And make them disappear into thin air,

Just like that.

Realisation

I haven't really gone bitter.
I just don't prefer sweetness much these days
Because I tend to go blind,
When it comes to separating salt from sugar.

Dull Days

Life has started to feel a lot like a closed glass jar, thrown into the vast ocean with nothing but the gigantic waves surrounding it and constantly knocking it down, restricting it from reaching the shore.

And it feels like I am stuck inside the glass jar, surrounded by nothing but my miseries and feelings of dejection and sorrow, being knocked down time and again by the blues, unable to reach the shore of felicity.

Real Strength

There is indeed strength in love,
But there is more so in heartbreak
For it makes you stronger.

Painful Art

An echo of all the unheard voices that wander
around in your head,

A caricature of all the unkempt feelings that you
try to hide,

A gory reminder of all the times you have fallen

And the striking pain of an old wound and a
thousand memories,

Together unravelling in the strokes of your old
paint brush

As you try to express what it is exactly that you're
feeling,

On the plain white canvas.

And at last, there it is,

A daunting masterpiece reflecting everything that
makes you, you.

Wounded, but still standing.

Strife

The way you took pride in your obscene glory of breaking a heart or two over your sixth glass of Glen Moray, even made a goddess as powerful as Eris envy you.

A Place You Can Call Home

If you keep on abandoning

The house that is built upon the foundation of promises,

You will never be able to find

A place that you can call home.

Novocaine Touch

Your touch felt absurdly calming initially,

As it numbed my pain.

But now I know that there is something as "too much"

Because your touch was fawningly deceiving.

It dulled not just my grief,

But each and every part of me,

Quite indiscriminatingly.

Bygones

It has been seventy-five days and five hours,
Since I last saw a tear dwelling from your swollen eye,
Since I last heard your voice getting caught up in your throat because you were too timid to say it out loud.

It has been seventy-five days and five hours,
Since you secretly slipped your hand into mine while no one was looking,
Since you placed my heart on the edge of your palm without even realizing the aftermath.

It has just been a matter of seventy-five days and five hours,
Since I cried a river of woe and flooded myself with dread,
Obliterating the best parts of myself,
And you did not even flinch.

It has just been seventy-five days and five hours of a mountain of overpowering emotions,
But it feels like an eternity of being ensnared in torment.

Threshold

I am not broken,
But that does not mean I won't break
For there is only so much that I can take.

Revelations

I am at the creek behind the limestone quarry,

The one which I tend to visit in my head,
whenever I need a getaway.

And as I am standing there barefoot,

I can feel the dirt on the back of my feet; the earth
is inviting me to rest into the extensiveness of its
roots.

I can hear the water calling out to me as it flows.

And so, I walk towards the stream.

I'm just standing there,

Lost in awe of the most banal wonders of nature.

I look down into the clear turquoise

And I can see innumerable rocks and stones trying
to catch my attention,

But my gaze is fixated on the water.

But it is upsetting, because even when I am
standing still,

The flow of the water makes it look like I am
shaking, my figure faltered.

It is almost as if the earth stems deep inside my
soul,

Which is why it is not fooled by my tough exterior; it can see me for who I am from the inside.

And that is frightening.

Maybe that's why I have never been the greatest admirer of water,

Not because it scares me by its immeasurable depth,

But because it can look into mine.

Unanswered Questions (I)

Is ignorance truly a bliss?

Or is there nothing else you can really do?

Unanswered Questions (II)

You remind me of my old wooden colour palette.

You have so many shades, it becomes difficult for me to pick my favourite.

You're like fresh crimson paint, the type that one extracts from wild berries, in its rawest and purest form.

But you're also like black, for your fury tends to stay unmatched.

There are so many shades of you, I cannot even begin to describe each one of them.

And what if these are merely the ones that I can see?

Is there more to you?

Reality Check

The paradox of reality, often becomes too harsh to handle

And so, we dwell into the comfort of our delusions.

The Predicament of Human Mind

It is not a bed of cactus as we have made it to be, all dark and twisted,

Filled with our apprehensions and nightmares.

It is instead, a bed of roses, because

Although there are thorns in roses which prick and hurt, its beauty remains still.

Love,

I like to perceive as a bed of roses,

The pulchritude of which makes you forget about the pinpricks of it all

Making even the plight, worth enduring.

Associating it with heartache only, is what blinds us

For we forget about the hearts that it mends,

The hurt that it heals,

And the contentment that it makes us feel.

The culprit of all the chaos and heartbreaks was never love,

For it only tends to fill our lives with more purpose.

The orchestration of it all,

The madness and the sadness,

Was ever only by the ill will of others.

Love was never meant to be bitter,

It is only us, who have made it so.

I Miss the Time I Never Had

I am sitting on the passenger's seat and watching the world pass me by,

The trees going back in a blurry motion

As I move forward

Towards an obscure destination of darkness.

Closer to the reality, perhaps.

The view reminds me of the way I used to watch time pass by,

How I did nothing to catch a hold of it

And how it effortlessly slipped out of my stained hands.

Maybe time mistook the smudged paint for blood

And left before it could even stay.

So, I dip my wooden brush in my tears

That flow in the reminiscence of every place I have yet to visit,

Of every heart I have yet to greet,

Every wound I have yet to feel,

And every memory I have yet to relive,

As an act of rebellion,

And paint yet another layer of my imagination,

Trying to capture glimpses of how things would have been

If only, I had time.

Why Do We Disregard the Consequences?

The seeds of sweet disaster were sown
In the garden of Eden,
Only to bear the forbidden fruit.
So, why do we still long for it,
Even when we know
How bitter the aftertaste is going to be?

Blue

I am swimming in an ocean of what I thought was our love,

But the weight of your betrayal is pulling me down,

And suddenly, I start to drown.

A Hysteric Episode

A part of me dies every day
As the sun rises and sets into the horizon.
And I lose myself every day,
Piece by piece,
Until I am fully unhinged.
My mind is full of cracks and crevices
That I fail to repair.
But I take comfort in the fact
That the day I meet death,
Is going to be the day I feel complete,
And whole.
For when I would be looking death in her eyes,
Life would regain its purpose,
And I will recover
All that I have lost of me.

Autumn Reminds Me of You

Autumn is a tricky weather,
Everything seems so bonny
But at the same time,
It is all so lifeless.
And you are like autumn.

Bonding Over Sorrow

I met the devil in my dream yesterday. He swayed and danced as he rejoiced his pain. I could certainly learn a thing or two from him; sometimes it feels like my life is filled with empty spaces and I don't know what to do about that, maybe I too could celebrate my anguish away. He told me he was best friends with death. He even admitted he felt like an outcast, with everyone obsessing over God; they used to be friends too. And all my life, I have felt like one too. Maybe we could get along.

Memories Trailing Down My Eyes

Your mellow gaze is leaving a trail of memories
In my sore eyes, every time I look around,
I find a part of you being projected
Through my hazy vision.

Rage

I keep playing the same record by The Velvet Underground

Again, and again

Because I broke all the others in a cobalt frenzy.

My anger is blue too.

The Perpetual Truth

I painted the mace with shades of pastel

To make it look less terrifying.

But that did not make it any less dangerous.

After all, one can only ever change the true nature of someone.

Façade

I held back my tears, choking on them
And letting out a silent sniffle.
It was the loudest cry for help that I could have let out,
Its quietness,
Wandering in my head
And slipping into my eyes.
I couldn't hold it back anymore.
But I loathed pity.
So, I channelled my sorrow into fury,
And burst into a fit of rage.
I failed to hold back my rather uncontrollable emotions
Yet again,
But I succeeded into making you see what I wanted you to,
Yet again.

A Terrible Influence

The people whose tears you try to wipe
Also happen to be the ones whose tears you have shed.
Your mind is a sinner's home,
And your rotten intentions feed your soul.
I can see through your tattered truths
And crowded lies.
If only, the others could see it too.
I can only hope they do someday,
And see you for who you truly are,
A sorry excuse for a naïve person.

Midnight Confrontations with Myself

I am laying down on the cold floor

As a trail of emptiness cascades down my left cheek.

I can feel your skin touching someone else's scars

And your thumb running circles

On the back of somebody else's palm.

And that used to pierce a hole through my dishevelled heart

Every time I used think about it.

But no more; I feel calmly arid.

My eyes are sore from swiping through our memories

Which are not ours anymore.

I don't even feel sick when I think about you anymore,

I simply feel nothing.

Zoning Out

I crack my bruised knuckles for the sixth time
As I zone out for the tenth time.
The reality is slipping by my vision
And I don't want to snap back to the world.
I am sipping on my tears
As I slowly spiral through a clementine fear
Of everything that I will have to face
As soon as I shake my head,
Vigorously blink my eyes,
And snap back to reality.

I Dream About Death

I go to sleep every night
So that I can meet death in my dreams.
The unbridled content
In romanticising death
As it approaches me
On a cold summer night,
Is outrageously beautiful,
And is also
Why I go to bed every night
Full of vigour.

Goodbye Darkness

I set a scalding fire to the bones of our love,
Which were once unbreakable.
The ash sparkled with sheer nothingness,
Just like star dust.
I put some on the edge of my palm,
Where my heart used to be,
And I scattered the ash
In the river of my unrequited love.

HOPEFUL REMINDERS

(a reminder, that no matter how dark your days get, there are always going to be better days waiting for you ahead)

You have you

Perhaps the best gift you could grant yourself with

Is that of love and acknowledgement

For fighting so many battles

And standing your ground

Even after being wounded.

Perhaps that is what you exactly need,

To take a break from beating yourself up

And giving yourself some time to heal.

A New Day

The sky broke down,

Only they weren't tears this time

Because it wasn't crying for help anymore.

It was washing down all the scars,

Cleaning up the wounds that once seemed everlasting.

But they were not.

It wasn't facile,

As it took the earth to tear up,

The ferocious wind to take a stroll through the whole city,

And the sun to stop blazing and disappear

To make way

For the clouds to take over the day,

And to look the atrocious misery in the eye,

Only to bid its farewell, once and for all.

What The "little things" Mean

The reverberating sound of all the atrocities of my life rings inside my ears, that are already tired

Of hearing the incessant sound of all the plight.

And although that sound is as disturbing as that of scraping metal,

Its emanation is rather different,

Quite biblical.

Maybe because it continues to be a relentlessly beautiful reminder

Of not only the sorrow,

But the strength that comes along with it,

The aftermath of enduring the hurt,

The silver-lining behind every storm that has passed

And the fact, that every storm does pass.

Perhaps that is one of the most amusing parts of human mind,

How even after putting it through complete burnout,

It puts up with every fight, in some way or the other.

And our hearts,

Oh, the sheer beauty of it,

Of how the perception of a broken heart, never stops one from beating.

The Notion of Beauty

The grey from the factory smoke popped out starkly in the pallidly invigorating blue sky and I stopped dead in my tracks as my eyes captured the scene. It was almost as if the collision of the tragic grey with the silent blue was a site to behold, weirdly entrancing. But it wasn't actually. It was as mundane as rain from a murky sky, but as soothing as the first raindrop hitting your skin. Funny how the most peculiar things catch your attention, rendering the definition of beauty quite futile; not only because of the obvious, that what might be beautiful to me, might not come off as amiable to you, but because of the fact that I would never perfectly be able to explain why it replicates the idea of beauty to me, and you would never really be able to understand either.

And so, I beg you to shield your idea of beauty and keep it close to your heart for as long as forever happens to be, because when the nights get too loud, it is going to be exactly these precious notions that wander around in your head, that will sing a lullaby of splendour to your heart and put it to a peaceful sleep.

Still Standing

The Persians did not hesitate to demolish the Parthenon

And loot it of its beauty.

They burned it down from its roots

And almost every other structure at the Acropolis.

And ever since,

The Greeks have been building all that they were robbed of,

Their home, and their hope.

But even after being completely destroyed,

The Acropolis has never stopped being everything that it stood for,

A citadel, a religious site, and a home to the kings and the gods.

It has been revived and rebuilt regardless of the colossal damage

And it continues to thaw every single heart

That has been wrenched out of love and hope by its eccentric beauty.

Broken, is indeed beautiful.

And so, I resuscitate my heart for the thousandth time

After it gets crushed and broken again

And I shall keep picking it up, piece by piece, time and again.

How it manages to make you smile, after the brutality it has witnessed,

I will never know.

But what I do know is that not once has it stopped beating,

Regardless of the hurt,

And so,

I owe this to my heart, to the blood that flows in my veins,

To not give up on it, because it never did either.

Music

My mind is a music box and there is a beautiful ballad playing on loop,

Keeping my thoughts at bay, and granting me peace every day.

Sweet Solitude

The enthralling scent of the French lavender fusing itself with the sweet air, creating a trance. The sky looking like a white canvas, with patches of blue smudged all over it.

The sound of the hummingbirds sitting on the enormous tree behind the cottage murmuring to each other.

Life blossoming from the rugged earth just three miles from my feet.

And there it goes, the shrieking kettle breaking my chain of thoughts and diverting my attention.

Keeping the back door open, I step inside the kitchen and start pouring out the hot liquid in the indigo ceramic cup with tiny designs in white on it.

Putting the kettle on the butcher block countertop and taking the cup in my hand, I walk out of the kitchen.

The warmth of the cup settling on my cold palms and the breeze gently touching my face brings me back to the exact moment I was pulled away from.

Bringing my face closer to the cup, I could feel the aroma spiralling through my nostrils to my head.

As soon as the tea touches my scabbed lips, I close my eyes in reminiscence and my lips turn into an expanding grin.

Drawing a deep breath, I open my eyes and saunter towards the field of the fetching lavenders.

And there I was, standing barefoot in the middle of the vast field with the fragrance and beauty of nature taking over my body and my spirit,

Grazing me with its beatific touch and reminding me of how life is so much more than a means to simply exist.

Rain

The overcast sky has a tinge of lilac in it.

And I incline my head out of the window of the moving car. It feels like one of those cliché movies, as I rest my head on the windowpane, only I anticipated it to be lighter, not with my heart so heavy and my mind so dreary.

And as the car is moving forward, my mind is racing in the opposite direction, tracing back the past.

Suddenly, the water droplets start hitting my skin. And as it starts to dampen, I close my eyes, and wait for the magic of rain to unravel.

I have always loathed monsoon, but it felt different tonight. It was as if I could finally understand all those, who love the rain.

Focus

I am learning to embrace my scars and my flaws

Instead of mocking them.

I am trying to be grateful for all that I am

Instead of sulking over all that I could have been.

I am trying to become a better version of myself than I was yesterday

Instead of wishing to be the best version of somebody else.

More than anything else,

I am trying.

My Resolve

I am in the paradise of a sweet fire that burns inside my mind

And its warmth is what shelters me

Not only from my own cold thoughts,

But from the icy stares of other people's minds too.

But its tenacity does not stop there,

For it burns a part of me every time I even think about giving up,

Reminding me of how I am not to put out these flames of ferocity.

And how I wouldn't be able to, even if I tried.

The Charisma of Winter

The best part of my day
Is neither the crisp early morning
Nor the cosy late night.
It is only the beautiful evening,
When the sun is about to set,
But is too generous to disappear right away.
So, it sticks around for a while,
And lets me soak myself in its tranquillity.
The way light welcomes itself into my room,
And slowly disappears
As the night is about to take over,
Is what fuels energy into my soul.
The fact that I would be able to witness the sky in a new element every day
Is oddly enough, what keeps me going.

The Wilderness

I lie down in the forest of my mind,
Where the sky shrouds my thoughts
And the leaves of the grapevine creep over my skin,
Where the sweet scent of the wet mud
Infuses with the gentle wind
And makes me feel at home.
In here, the deer is sitting beside the lion,
And is listening to his melodious roar.
Nature really is too generous.
And it is so, not only in my head
Because everywhere I go,
It leaves a part of its eternal beauty with me
Forever.

Let Go

You need to let yourself go. Life is not always a game of chess and you do not need to calculate and analyse every move you make.

Sometimes, just sometimes, you have to do what you feel like doing and what you believe will bring you closer to yourself.

Unlike the game of chess, where you lose if you make even one flawed move, that is not the case in real life.

It's not one wrong move and game over, instead, it is one wrong move, and start over.

Quaint Recollections

I wrap myself with strings of you,
And find fabrics of you in me
Every time I have a tear in my eye,
Because I laughed too much.
I hope you find me too
In your smile someday,
When you find a cloth
That makes you feel the warmth
That my arms did.

Courage

My courage used to be bottled up in a mason jar
Whose lid I could open only under tremendous pressure.
I keep taking tiny chunks out of it every now and then.
But as I fill my fist with my dying courage,
It falls out of the empty spaces, like grains of sand.
So, I search for its remnants in myself
As the beat of paranoia throbs in my chest,
Asking me to save as much as I can,
So that I don't run out of my timid courage.
I think about breaking the glass of the jar more than I sleep,
But my fears creep inside my mind,
What if that shatters what's left of my courage too?
I need more power for executing that.
But do I have that?
And the only way to answer that was to break the glass.
So, I did.

My courage isn't imprisoned by anything anymore.

It smells like the spirit of Kratos

As its ethereal emanation takes over me.

My courage is not timid anymore,

Instead, it is the mighty depiction

Of how the God of strength bestowed a part of his heart

To my soul,

Making its roots,

Even deeper with undying courage.

A Lasting Imprint

I will wrap your presence in an iridescent seashell of my love and faith

And preserve it like a giddy child,

Who gets captivated by that one rock on the beach

And keeps it close to her for the rest of her life,

Almost as if it is a part of her.

And as I will bore your presence into me,

Your absence would never make me feel alone,

For you would always be there anyways.

Scars

Another wildflower bloomed on my body yesterday.

I used to tell myself they were weeds I needed to get rid of.

But this meadow of wildflowers,

That I very conveniently used to frown upon,

Is simply, a pretty significance of who I am.

Coffee and Books

I will paint you with big words and small punctuations
And write a story narrating us,
Portraying you lost in your element,
And me getting lost in you.
I will highlight you with bold letters
And emphasise your riveting aura
In such a way that even the reader
Would be overwhelmed by the wordy emotions.
I will capture your dulcet smile into rhetorical questions
That will linger on my sleeve
For as long as my words do,
And treasure it as I would my favourite book.
I will infuse your smell in the pages of my book,
So that every time I turn a page,
I would never run short of you.

And as I fill my book with recollections and pieces of you,

I will cherish it and hold it close to my heart.

And when I am done reading,

I will softly place it beside my coffee mug

So that every time I need a refill and grab my mug,

I would get a quick look at it too.

Besides, it would be a sin to mix it with any other book I have,

For this one would be monumentally special.

Gingham Love

In a town far away from my grief,
I found a raging love,
Where two parallels meet
Only to celebrate their differences,
And being sated with the fact,
That they only met,
To part their ways.

Be Proud of Yourself

You did not come all this way
Just to let loose of hope
And mope.
So, take pride in your bruises
For they are a reminder
Of every hindrance
That you have tackled,
And all that you have achieved.

Trying to Live More

As every moment passes me by,
I realise that never is there going to be
Another one, just like this.
And so, I try to laugh a little louder,
Fight a little less,
And live a little more,
In the hope of making the best
Out of that moment
Because the universe is too hard working
To not curate each and every one of our experiences,
At least slightly different than the previous one.
And it would be a tiring shame
If I wasted any moment at all.

The Perfect Combination of Bittersweet

Our love is like a Shakespearean nightmare
Where unnecessary blood is shed
And sturdy sacrifices are made,
And yet we still manage to escape the fissure
That has been gaped inside our hearts.
And that is why,
I will preserve our love
The way Victorian monuments are preserved,
Because I can never get enough
Of its intricately beautiful architecture
And our love,
Is more or less
Built in a similar way.

So, I will keep the key to our love safe
By always wearing it around my neck,
I will never take all the tears shed for granted
Instead, I will save them in a jar

Which I will carry around with me
For as long as there is life in my body,
Because after every tantrum gifted
And every whisper that turned into a scream,
Our love still manages
To bring out the best of us.

The Stars

The stars have bleached this dark world
With hope and light,
Way more than the moon ever could
Because although the moon is luminously beautiful,
The stars burn
And only for us,
So that whenever we get cornered
By our deepest and darkest fears,
The stars would grant us a safe space
In the light which they radiate,
By setting themselves on fire.

A Feral Escape

I am a castle of perfectly timed unfortunate events.
The wounded raven comes to sit on my windowpane
Every day, and keeps me company
As I daydream aimlessly.
The mist surrounding, makes it difficult
For me to see through people
And so, I put my blind faith in peril
Yet again.
There is a broken bridge nearby
Where detached souls are listening to Hozier
And lovers are blaming each other
For their eternal misery instilled state.
But amidst this Aphrodite orchestrated havoc,
I take solace in the fact
That the abandoned library
Whose doors lead to an altered reality,
Is always welcoming me, with its arms wide open,
Allowing me to wallow
In the luxury of literature.

Healing

My lungs are a garden
Filled with the most exquisite flowers
But I burn them down to the ground
And inhale the sweet smoke.
I should be choking on love
But I only run out of breath
Every now and then; I am living on borrowed air.
The cry of a lunatic in love
Is what keeps me up at night.
But as soon as our lips collide
Even the ash feels blissful
For your lips bear
The taste of an invigorating hope.
It warps the sight of the flowers I killed
And I can see a bed of snowdrops
Being planted
In the abyss of my heart.

Undefeated

For every time
That woe visits your home,
I will be on the doorstep,
Waiting to defeat
Its arsenal of gruesome nightmares
Along with the most powerful cavalry
Of all time,
Filled with soldiers
Who are deep in love.

Life in Death

The sky would come to visit me
On my death bed
And the clouds will sink their claws
Deep into my mind,
Thereby wrenching it out
Of its abhorrent ways of being.

The day I die,
My soul would be mounted
On the pedestal of a peaceful adventure.

My pale bones would subside
Into the flesh of this exuberant earth
And the grim reaper would be dancing
On the renaissance of my spirit.

The neglected river
Would gush in the remembrance
Of the teal splashing
On my scraggy palm.

And on my death,
My meek eyes would witness
Hades enrapturing me
With the punishment of love.

Change

The first sip of liquor
Had now turned into the first sip
Of freshly brewed coffee in the morning.
The sun felt like it enveloped me into its warmth
Instead of poking me with its blazing rays.
The smell of the ocean did not make me nauseous anymore,
It instead felt serene.
I felt more ready than ever,
Ready to drive towards a new challenge,
A change perhaps, from my despondent way of living,
A chance, to break open from the chain of excuses and doubts
And jump right into the ocean of opportunity.

I Sold My Soul to The Sky

The charcoal sky is melting slowly

And my soul with it.

My skin does not feel uncomfortable anymore,

My eyes are tucked away in a reverie,

And my bones are resting in the hollow casket

Which is my body.

I am rendered as an empty vessel

And my spirit is soaring high with the sullen clouds.

Alas, peace has found me.

Not Flawless

You don't need to accept your flaws forcefully
As an act of fate.
You need to love them,
Embrace them,
Even learn from them if you may,
But your flaws only make you more you.
After all, they are an essential part of who you are.

Take the Risk

You keep turning a blind eye
To that glimmering ray of hope
That keeps nudging your shoulder
To just take a look at it.
But you don't
Because you are scared
Of that light turning into darkness.
But how will you ever know
If you never reach out to it?
The result might or might not disappoint you
But not knowing, will be worse
Because regret will kill you.

You Will

You will leave behind all those things
That you bear all alone and don't talk to anybody about.
You will win the battles that you fight by yourself
And even if you lose, you will never lose yourself.
You will rise above all your misgivings and doubts
That you feel bring you down.
And you will always find yourself and have yourself
No matter how many times you get lost in the way.

Smile

Your smile is a menace to all those who serve the hollows,

The slaves of a haunted fate,

Too afraid to bear the sin of being happy.

So, let your contagious smile

Reach the dullest and the loneliest corners of the world

And let it be an extension of help,

A leap of faith even,

To those who have submitted to the rather drab wonders of life.

Let your smile seep through the dark debris of life

Under which people are stuck

And let them taste the sweetness of light.

Don't supress your tears,

Only smile a little bit more

And let it illuminate not only your life,

But also, that of those around you.

The Way of Life

At the end of the dark tunnel
Filled with a woeful commotion,
Await the mountains of joy,
Surrounded with a placid fog.
The air is filled with a sincere hope there,
A reminder perhaps,
That life is never always blithe
But it is definitely never always bitter either.

I Can Feel My Heart Smile

The faint sunlight streaking through the frosty window, punctured my skin with warmth.

The first ray of light on a cold winter morning has to be one of the most underrated gestures of affection portrayed by nature. And for that, I am utterly grateful.

We are two worlds apart, but to think that you would be squinting your eyes in the heat of the same sun, my heart smiles at the thought.

And as nature engulfs us into a petrichor hug, I will know that you are safe in the arms of the same sky that I am, even if you are a world away from me.

A Tale of Strength

For every time
An unknown and unwanted touch
Was pierced upon my skin,
It felt obnoxiously uncomfortable,
As if this body that I am residing in,
Is not my own,
And I am paying rent to everybody else
Because they think it belongs to them.
For every time
I narrated my side
And it was shrugged off in derision,
I felt like abandoning this body
That I used to consider as my shrine,
Because I couldn't think of any other way
To stop the hurt.
But regardless of every time
That my experiences were invalidated,
And I was forced to question my own self,

Regardless of every blame that was pinned upon me,

And I was driven to change myself,

I am proud of myself for putting up with all those times,

For staying strong,

For realising my worth,

And for never changing myself.

And you should be too.

You are more than your doubts

And what society claims you to be,

You are strong,

You are worth the best,

And you are the best.

A Date with Nature

I could spend hours sitting on the damp grass
Surrounded by the compelling silence
And the barren night sky.
Not a star in sight,
Yet it looks as fetching as it always does.
Crickets chirping,
Sending secret messages to the moon
And the wind delivering them to her.
I could sit here
For as long as the sky would want me to.
I could spend hours here
All by myself
And would never get bored.

Victory

The paper is stained by my nosebleed
From yesterday morning
And my words have become bloodier,
But my emotions remain fortified
And untarnished still.
It is like a battle cry; I can hear my words calling out to me,
Chanting in rhythm with my thoughts,
And mightily yelling at me
That I will thrash my demons
And that I will emerge triumphant.

My Survival Kit

I was once asked to state the necessary constituents of a survival kit.

I thought about it for a good couple of minutes but all I could think of was her, about how she was the one without whom I wouldn't be able to survive, about how I wouldn't need a medical kit because she could take away all the hurt, all the agony, she always does.

I could only think about how a flashlight would not be necessary because she was jovial enough to make even the darkest times shine as bright as the sky does on a starlit night.

All I could think of was how I did not need to be dependent on a survival kit because I had her, my support system, the only one I would ever need to survive, my mother.